# I CAN BE A

# BAKER

By Dee Lillegard

Prepared under the direction of Robert Hillerich, Ph.D.

With special thanks to Wayne Stoker, Master Baker and Culinary Arts Instructor,
Laney Community College, Oakland, California

 CHILDRENS PRESS ®

CHICAGO

Library of Congress Cataloging in Publication Data

Lillegard, Dee.
  I can be a baker.

  (I can be series)
  Includes index.
  Summary: Briefly describes the training and jobs of
bakers.
  1. Baking—Vocational guidance—Juvenile literature.
2. Bakers and bakeries—Juvenile literature.
[1. Baking—Vocational guidance. 2. Bakers and bakeries.
3. Vocational guidance 4. Occupations] I. Title II. Series.
TX769.L485 1986   664'.752'023    85-27976
ISBN 0-516-01892-2

# PICTURE DICTIONARY

baker

dough

ingredients

yeast

barrel mixer

pastries

chemist

# ACME BAKING SCHOOL

PIES BREAD

stations

laboratory

hand shop

tunnel oven

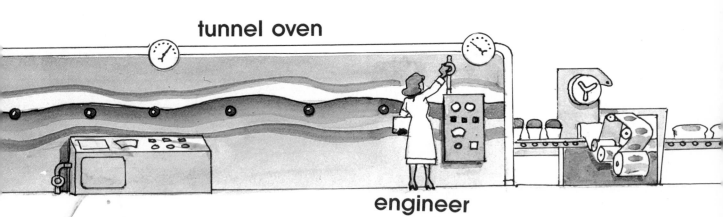

engineer

factory

When you bake at home, you learn many of the skills
that professional bakers use on the job.

Small bakeries bake their goods early every morning.

Many people like to bake. They like to make cookies and breads and delicious pastries. But a baker is someone whose job is to bake. Bakers make many different foods that people can buy to eat.

pastries

baker

These rolls are set in a rack while the
yeast grows and makes them rise.

Bakers go to baking school to learn their trade. They learn about different kinds of flour and sugar. They learn about yeast.

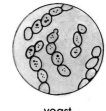

yeast

Yeast is a very tiny plant that is mixed in with dough. When the yeast grows, it causes the dough to rise. This is what keeps bread from being flat and hard.

dough

Students in a baking school work in teams in each station.

**ingredients**

**laboratory**

Bakers have to know arithmetic. They must learn how to measure ingredients accurately.

A baking school has a laboratory. The laboratory, or lab, has different areas or stations.

Left: Students making a mandarin orange cream pie
Right: Apple pies, and pie crusts waiting to be filled

Baking students learn certain things at each station. They learn to make pies and turnovers at one. They bake breads and biscuits at another.

stations

9

Left: Baking instructor shows students how to cut a cream pie.
Right: Mixing dough can be a hands-on experience.

There may be as many
as ten stations in a lab.
Every student gets to work
at every station.

Dough mixer dumps out a huge ball of dough that will soon become four hundred loaves of bread.

Some bakers work in factories. They work with huge machines that mix and bake.

Other bakers work in small bakeries called hand shops. In hand shops, the work is done mostly by hand.

In a hand shop, the bakers work together as a team. They move fast.

hand shop

Loaves of cinnamon-raisin bread are tipped out of their baking pans. Next, they are covered with a sugary glaze. Finally, a cutting machine cuts each loaf into slices.

The baker will place the top half of the cake on top of the delicious filling.

A birthday cake with a filling inside is usually made by three or four people. First, many cakes are placed on a bench. The bakers move around the bench. One slices the cakes. One fills them.

Look at all these colors of frosting! The baker puts a different color in each pastry bag and squeezes it out in beautiful designs.

Another baker stacks the slices. And another decorates the cakes.

This way, several cakes can be made in a few minutes.

This bakery makes a thousand loaves of bread a minute.
Left: Bread on its way to the slicer. Right: Hamburger buns
on their way to the cooler

For hundreds of years,
baking was done only by
hand. Today, machines
produce millions of
cookies, crackers, buns,
and loaves of bread.

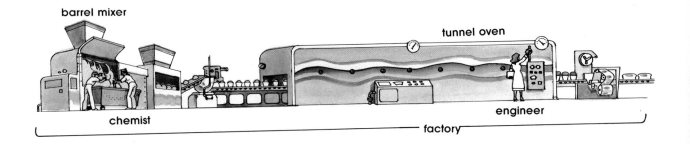

barrel mixer

tunnel oven

chemist

engineer

factory

Factories can produce many baked foods in a few seconds.

Many factory bakers are chemists or engineers. They must understand baking machinery, such as barrel mixers and tunnel ovens.

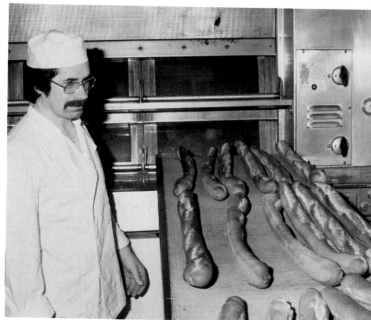

Long loaves of French bread

Tunnel ovens are very
big. They can hold as
many as a hundred
loaves of bread at once.
One baker puts the
bread dough in the front
of the oven. Another

baker takes the baked bread out at the end of the oven.

Hand shop bakers believe that people can make better baked goods than machines can. Hand shop bakers take special pride in what they make and sell. They believe their baked goods are fresher and tastier.

Different stages of bread-making at a factory bakery:
Mixing dough (above), weighing flour (opposite page), and
checking pans to see if they are full of dough (below)

Bakers work different
hours than many other
workers do. Most factories
run all day and all night,
every day of the week.
Factory bakers work in
shifts. They may work a
morning shift, an evening
shift, or a night shift.

Left: Handmade bread, freshly baked. Right: After the dough rises, it is punched down and shaped into loaves to rise again.

Some hand shops open early in the morning. They serve fresh doughnuts and pastries

Everything at this bakery is made from natural ingredients, with no chemicals added.

to people on their way to work. Their bakers come to work very early. The doughnuts and pastries must be ready on time.

There are many different jobs for bakers. Very few bakers do everything.

There are bakers who specialize in desserts. There are bakers who make fine candies. There are bakers who make only breads or pastries. Some bakers make their living baking cookies.

Above: Making sweet rolls (left). Glazing fruit tarts (right)
Below: Cutting out doughnuts (left). Decorating a cake (right)

Above: A team of bakers in a bakery kitchen. Below: Doughnut dough is loaded into a machine that drops the doughnuts into a deep fryer.

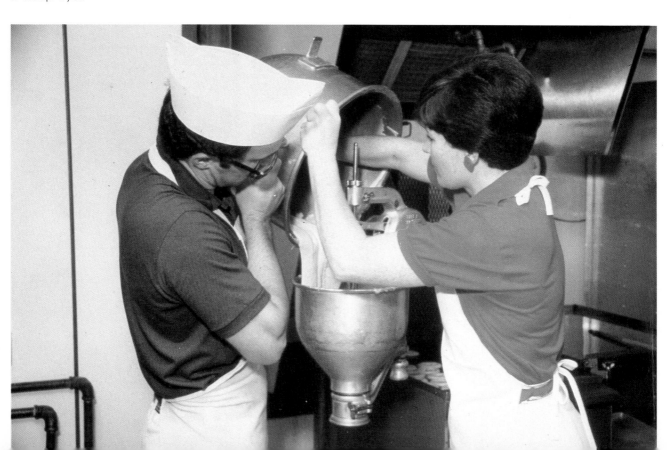

But all bakers must like what they are doing. They must be able to move from one thing to another quickly. They must be able to get along well with one another and work as a team. And they must take pride in doing their best at all times.

Above: Loading ingredients into a mixer (left). Huge
containers of ingredients (right). Below: Spraying pastries
with water to make them crispy when they bake

Left: Removing dough from mixing bowl. Right: Weighing ingredients

Baking is hard work. But
bakers think it's worth it—
especially when
someone says, "Mmm!
This is good!"

## WORDS YOU SHOULD KNOW

**bakery** (BAY • kur • ee)—a shop or factory where breads and baked desserts are made

**biscuit** (BISS • kit)—a small quick-baked bread, usually round and flat

**chemist** (KEM • ist)—a scientist who knows about substances and how they behave

**dough** (DOH)—a mixture of flour, water or milk, and other ingredients

**doughnut** (DOH • nut)—a small, ring-shaped cake

**engineer** (en • juh • NEER)—a scientist who understands engines or machines and how they work

**ingredients** (in • GREE • dee • unts)—all the parts that something is made of

**pastries** (PAISS • treez)—sweet baked goods made from dough

**shift** (SHIHFT)—a regular time period for work

**specialize** (SPEH • shul • ize)—to do just one kind of work

**turnover** (TURN • oh • ver)—a filled pastry made by folding half the dough over the other half

**yeast** (YEEST)—a tiny plant used in making dough. When the yeast grows, the dough rises up.

## INDEX

## PHOTO CREDITS

## ABOUT THE AUTHOR

Dee Lillegard (born Deanna Quintel) is the author of over two hundred published stories, poems, and puzzles for children, plus *Word Skills*, a series of high-interest grammar worktexts, and *September to September, Poems for All Year 'Round*, a teacher resource. Ms. Lillegard has also worked as a children's book editor and teaches writing for children in the San Francisco Bay Area. Next to writing, food is her favorite subject.